LUMINISM
poems by Jim Hanson

FENNVILLE, MICHIGAN 2016

copyright 2016 by Jim Hanson

2907 63rd St
Fennville MI 49408
http://jimhanson.org

Some of these poems appeared in *Victorious Photographs Broadsides*, *Dental Floss*, *Mag City*, *4 3 2 Review*, *Hard Press* postcard series and *Nicolas et Magdeleine.*

"I believe in religion not magic or science I believe in society
as religious both man and society as religious"

Charles Olson, *The Maximus Poems* (III. 55)

COOL STARS

Cool stars send us light
from years ago. Plants
wave their leaves so slowly
we can't see them move.

On the dark screen there
is a sudden flash. Leaves
blow aside & lids open.
Ashes fly into eyes.

Leaves wave across the
screen. Ashes are taken
up into the wind as stars
blink like eyelids.

Eyelids close as glass
stars fly across
the screen like leaf
ashes in the wind.

A cool flash & the screen
turns to ashes. Suddenly
leaves appear behind the
glass & the stars darken

DEAR ARTIST
for Alice Notley

Dear Artist

   How it must be
  strange to find
     these uncanny resemblances
in your children
    "you & you & you" all around
and in each a little particle of "me"
   colors, touches, and thoughts
       of a new person
like all the things of your life
     the events placed gently
into the form of the works
   angels, moves, early light
      and the eternal orange
juice
  the season when refrigerators bump up the stairs
Bob Dylan (a good friend)
      and Sam Cooke
All this flies through my mind
    as the leaves scatter before me
      across the stones
as I walk to school
    the words of my work
       all over my
notebooks
Words move through my head:
    descent, succession, kinship, marriage
     as I share a kiss
over the pastries
     basement coffeeshop
I look for my coincidences in books, music
faces

    and visions of the everyday
                                          For me as for you
Perception and ardor are the sweet facts
and dear America
                    the background to your easy grace

POEM ("YOU ARISE FROM SLEEP...")

You arise from sleep in your domicile
Breathing. Actually it keeps us alive
Us mammals. Everything does: the air,
Apples, flakes for breakfast, orange liquid and
The sudden welling-up of brightness.
Really the best. Really a calm
Style. Ice chunks fall into street.
My head fills with light when I stand up. Really
Snowing. Clouded windows. Outside the promise
Of more cold air. The gleam of your wet skin
And the tiny flowers surrounding the place
You sleep. These are important. As important as
The atmosphere or the rays from our star.
These things keep me alive and happy. Naturally
Breathing, thinking, wanting to know all about you.

POEM ("MORE MEAT AND SUGAR")

more
meat and sugar
will find its way into the hands of America's greedy housewives
for the US deportment
of agriculture has given we've heard "so we've heard" house
"so we've heard" "so we've heard" wives a piece of the hardest
earned meat in history
maim aim aim bang bang bang bang "so we've heard"

THE INSTRUCTIONS

We thought the wash of the sea was turning, and our feet trailed off in the wet sand,
We thought the wrath of the day was upon us, but we were wrong.
We went out into the flower garden and opened our satchels
Inside--the Instructions. We opened them. They were white and huge
Unlike anything we'd seen before.
The words, too, they were new. I remember some of them
"A convenient form. A mode of expression. Financial reverses, domestic infelicity and the like"
We wore our anoraks outside, carefully carrying
The Instructions along with us.
To the center of the formal garden
We walked, a giant sheet of paper trailing behind us
In the breeze. The sand swirls were crisp.
In the early light
We knelt to read the Instructions

** INSTRUCTIONS **

1. Attach a string to the center of the garden bed. Now, another star point. Next a star point and the circle. And your star is complete.

2. Fill the desert grotto with molten glass to replace the water.

3. Mechanical animals can be made to bend down and drink from the pool while tiny electric lights flash against a black backdrop.

POEM IN PRAISE OF A CAR

Der Abend des Morgens kommt wie die Dämmerung zurück

The morning's evening returns to dusk
the halflight penetrates as far as here
Construction fence creaks in the wind
proclaiming bloody winter evening
and the sun sets disturbingly
through the massive clouds
that people create in the process of
keeping themselves warm

Their little houses are worlds
that line the streets down which I walk
like a halfdark shadow halfcomprehending
what I see   I think only of comfort
comfort that will come to me when I step inside
the door of the little world

The cars too are worlds
the motors run except when plagued by 'car trouble'
when they sputter or even fail to turn over
demanding to be left alone

They're only machines
can't operate like we do
forever going on and on
except for when we sleep

They must be turned on and off
Ignition must be sparked to make them run
and since their natural state is blissful silence
and the immobility of metals and fluids
they do not want to carry us to work today, no!

And so after twice trying to make my car start
by turning the little key
I said to myself, "I know a secret--
This car will not start today, too bad,
noble mechanism."
And I think of the times the car has stopped
although it is a good car it is tired metal
it has stopped in traffic too
mostly when I didn't care for it
let one of its precious lifebloods run low

But today I stride down the street
away from the car
Subzero temperatures don't bother me
I'm warmly dressed
I'm happy, even, the car is happy
it will start another day, a warmer one
I'd even whistle if I knew how
walking those twelve blocks to work
when crossing a street
a phrase comes into my head and
it is another one
the morning's evening returns like dusk
Der Abend des Morgens kehrt wieder wie das Halbdunkel

SPACIOUSNESS

Most of a moon hung, limpid, in complete blackness. Night breezes of summer totally shake a plenitude of leaves. Wave swirls of this sound follow. Shadows of small oaks and firs are fixed, sharply outlined against the grass's gray luminescence. The distant doppler of the highway not out of place. Noble trucks are the large, large tables of the hand, and headlights a radiant flux, kinetic as rayon.

Behind the earth's ribs the shining would be a town. Heartbeat refrain of iron wheels on rails and lonely train whistle coming to a crossing echo off junked cars, rustling weeds, silent roads. The creek mumbles over its rocks, under the old stone trestle. The planet's night is endless, in all directions immense, terrestrial, worldwide

Ah Space AH SPACE

SHAGBARK

let us create
for ourselves
a varied coast
they said
to themselves
one day on
the level marshes
upon which to build anew
so peninsulas & parks
were laid down
boulevards & towers
took shape
along the lake
a city
it was there
I was born
while bird songs
intensified
distant dogs barked
& children
across the way
shouted
& called

among the trees
I was taken
to remember only
the grey branches
stretching up
the shagbark hickory
majestic, giant
cosmic in scope
from the top of which
on a clear day

you could see
above the other trees
leaves slapping
each other
noisily below
moving breezes
creating sound
you could see
the Fox River
stretching away
a brown curl
far beyond
the slight hills
& leftover woods
of the place
where once the glaciers
met the plains
called the midwest

I was taken there
but I grew
& the shagbark
who had been there
for centuries
making the place
his own
whose huge
handlike leaves
yellowed in fall
& whose trunk
was plated
with strips of bark
jutting out
like wooden petals
the shagbark
blessed me

& sent me on my way
to change & grow
the shagbark
blessed me one time
& it is enough

SJOBERG'S

(1)

A maverick wind sweeps Allamakee
county & leaves an aura of
mandolins in country intricacy,
of all sounds the most precise.
Iowa mandarins drive out to see
their country places in a
shifting rain, still
as glass, an approximation of stasis
which means no movement.
No movement is as random as dust's
blowing down the Upper Iowa
Valley, this very moment, brooming
& cleaning, sweet July emerges intimately--
A maverick wind sweeps Allamakee

(2)

I am in a room
& the ghost of John Sjoberg sits across from me
across the table from me, across the teacups
not his ghost but rather his presence
reserved & puffing clouds

                      MCDONALD'S TOBACCO

following tangles to their ultimate solutions
investigating evidence, expressing beliefs
in the vast magnitude of his speaking, his continuance
his talk is like kitestring
unraveled in his hands

                                ONE QT. "OLD STYLE"

there are secret places in the woods
he wishes to tell me of
he has shown me these places
but I have forgotten where they are
only to discover one of them today
when I went to Hickory Hill
& found a shagbark

                          ABADIE. PARIS

& ran down treacherous eroded pathways
& walked over green swards
& noticed whippoorwill calls
& tiny violets scattered underfoot
distant thunder, light rain
the flowering iowa bushes
some magic behind it all

                                    (Sjoberg's)

(3)

We speak of passenger pigeons
& dust. Audubon's painting
is there, a gift to him.
The pigeons, wing-blue in
jeweled innocence, numbered
and named in Latin. John
notes that the male feeds
the female & smiles. The birds
conjoin on a branch laden
with dying leaves. The dust,
he says, simply blows away

NY SKIES
for Steve Levine

you can watch the planes at night
if such is your pleasure
stars no longer being visible in cities
instead you watch these machines
eastbound to LaGuardia and Kennedy
westbound to Newark and beyond
and everywhere the glow
unmistakable
from the planes they realize
there are people down below
you are one of them
dart the helicopters ever so quickly
as on an electric-lit night in Manhattan?
will it ever stop?
this motion
trails across the dome
as real as humankind
nowhere it is silent
it is us, we are humming

THE APPRECIATION OF THE TEXT
for Allan and Cinda Kornblum

Manys the time I have sat across yr table & listened to you slowly declaiming some narrative from some where
& manys the time we were awestruck and laughing at some limited edition, specially bound in granite, reviewed in the pages
& manys the time we have shared poems with each other, reading them as they should be read, peaceably, cups of coffee before us
& manys the time that the third light of morning illuminated breakfast there, you and Cinda, myself, the variable others
& manys the time we've sat up late at night, working in the book factory, doing all the little tasks required to put the signatures together into a book, multiplied by the hundreds
& manys the time an after reading party sparkled around the board, poets & friends, imaginations going full tilt, with music around the corner, typewriter passing from collaborator to another in the living room
& manys the time we have left one by one to view the stars over darkened Iowa, the stream of interstate traffic, gentle planetary folds of West Branch
& manys the time I've enjoyed quiet dinner there with you both, garden fragrances rising in steam
& the many times we've spent together are like a text, to go over again & again, remembering
Textual variances, recurrences, changes, new motifs, returns to beginnings
& I am the text, reading itself, and I appreciate
I appreciate the many times I've shared
Your company
Your hospitality
Your viewpoints and your laughter

THE ORIGIN OF LANGUAGE

Languages arose
On all sides
& alphabets
Were chosen

FROM THE NEW WORLD
for Ralston Bedge

overhead, astern
the stars & streams of silent galaxies
a considerable beauty shining with heat
unfelt in this planet's cool evening
the ship plows on, unheard
with a sound like children whispering

the pleasant hidden fields
beyond the near coast
fall away, dark with sleep
invisible they are, through the tinted glass
beyond our power to add or detract

What we call the new world
is really a collection of spaces
Under a sky plastered with images
& leftover ideas. Each place is but a space
between borders traced by an unseen hand.
There is no place for love's body
in all of this. Love's body
seems distant in these states

when in the course of human events
the central interest of all unfolds
it becomes necessary

when it becomes necessary
it becomes us to speak
of the centerpiece to everyone living
& all that's contained by human emotions --
love's body, red star over China

the distant planets, the beings growing nearer

SIAM CAFE

One afternoon in Chicago, walking with my cool pal Arnie
down Lawrence Avenue Uptown where the L rattles over
a rundown looking neighborhood teeming with senior
citizens
The Aragon marquee featuring "Montrose" or "Los
Zapatistas"
We were looking for a Xerox machine to copy some poems
went to a bank
Stopped in at a Kresge's
I ate an eclair -- a weird object
Then, on Sheridan, stopped in the Siam Cafe
a nondescript restaurant where water is served in a tin bowl
by pretty Siamese waitresses
The menu is half Siamese and half English

They have the greatest food and that afternoon
we shared a Charcoal Chicken which is burned
barbequed chicken with dark flecks of sauce
and completely delicious
They also have the hottest sweet and sour pork
I've ever sampled, laden, as it is,
with thin strips of banana peppers
And also a very cheap fried rice with egg flecks

And for dessert -- candied water chestnuts
which look like cherry Jello chunks
floating in milk and ice cubes
After five minutes of eating this dessert
you have as much left as when you started to eat it
Ten minutes later, you give up, happily sated and piqued by
this treat,
leave a big tip and saunter down the summer street night

I've been in the Siam Cafe many times on fond visits

to my native city, and I recommend it highly to all
I wish I were there, being so hungry right now in Iowa
City room watching football –
                              I salute you, Siam Cafe --
you are unreal!

ON THE ACCIDENTAL MUSIC

Behind the sounds you hear everyday
the escaping gas, the puff of flame
lurks a music, daughter of chance
composed of cars in swift passage
radios, children shouting in the dark
an alarm, a clatter or a rumble
& the chants of the Vietnamese
on another floor, another continent.
You discover a ripple in the surface
behind the face of what you notice
that lets you hear these sounds:
blue formations in the busy zones
jazz, trucks & the shattering vibration
that's only aluminum foil being shaken

DOG RIVER NEWS

Suddenly dogs howled
and I knew there was such a thing as a breakthrough
the ice thawed, the stream coursed on
and when I looked across river, there was smoke in the willow grove
and wood fires among the trees in bud
I knew that people had come into the world to change everything
the location of the trees will change for their being here
the very course of the river will be different
Still in spring the ice floats downstream
the water is high, the earth wet with the snow of months past
and the river has no choice but to make its way onward
stone blue like it shall be

THE SINGLE BACKBONE COUNTRY

Outside the targets called cities
Away from the crowds walking shoulder to shoulder
Away from the bastards who breeze through the green light and leave you with the red
Away from the interstate, the symbol of no restrictions
The freedom you feel driving along, open road ahead
Planet's edge in the distance
Wind from an open window caressing your face

To walk along the interstate is a revelation of destruction
Dead animal comrades, the discarded packaging indicating the presence of humans' passage
To hitchhike down this road is to be one with the brothers on the ramps present and absent
It is also to be at the mercy of the cars which pass in an endless stream
Each guided by a free person
Away from all these things, a river continues downhill
Toward the sea
Which is far

The river centers a valley, a smiling visage, gentle slopes rolling
It is the cord that binds it together
The streams flow past the woods and into the fields
Joining it all into one
It is the single backbone country
So called by the original people
When they returned from their exile

It is a land of people who depend upon and support each other
As the body does itself
Or as a house stands, one stone, one beam, which holds it up
Or as the interplay of earth, sky, plants
Original animals and men was
One species supporting another
Food for the tribe

Our buffalo heritage is gone
Along with the virgin stands of forests
The weeds of the prairie

I wouldn't waste any tears on that

But we can inquire within
And know how much we've lost
Without knowing what we've lost

Some of it lives on in the country

The hills are still there
Indigenous birds mingle with those from elsewhere
People blissfully unaware which are which
As the songs blend with the rising of the sun

New trees introduced onto the continent
Give the land a new face
The trees planted in rows along country roads
And the streets of town
A contribution by some long dead farmer or another
Organizing the landscape to suit his own ideas of perfection

And indeed, the trees are perfect
Long colonnades of living wood on either side of the road
Paced evenly, the waving leaves meet directly overhead
The tunnel is alive

The cars pass over bridges and roads
Marks on the land which have changed everything
Curving down hills, black and gummy in the sun
They pretend to be endless stone surfaces

Cemeteries and parks, playgrounds and parking lots in the towns
Replace the old open spaces with new, unalterably changed ones
The country has many nerves now, many bones
Many tissues joining each to each
Yet somehow in the mind's glance it remains single, straightforward, clean and very new
The single backbone country
As seen long ago

Clouds blow in from nowhere
And the heat relaxes
The wind picks up the humid air
The light fades, the sky darkens

Everything is filled with the certainty of immediate change

Promises fulfilled, events become actual
The wind throws things around the streets
Curtains move inward, then, reversed are sucked against the screen
Like breath the movement, inhaling, exhaling
In the country the rows of corn and soybeans shake with relief
The trees at the edge of the field no longer keep silent
As the first drops of rain fall over the contours and folds of the earth
The sky is awesome and dark
A mass of clouds, an indistinct pattern
As the rain becomes more intense and washes down
Over the windshields of the cars headed west
The wipers carry it away endlessly

Over the sidewalks of the town, darkening
Over the windows
Onto the streets, down the gutters, into the culverts
Which carry the rain to the river
Goal of all precipitation
Center of the geography of this valley
The single backbone country
The world that is

Illimitable as a gentle curve
Sloping away towards the houses
Black angel
Spreads wings and arms
Over the tombstones and evergreens (one, dying, red as rust) in the graveyard
Peopling the green mounds broken by ancient trees

Her one arm extended outwards in a gesture of mercy
The other raised to the sky
The palm of retribution

Her place is here
She is great, unusual, for this city
Too small or too poor to have statues in public places
Lacking even the usual stone presidents and heroes

So she is a landmark
And people, each to each, relate a tale, that is, a legend

As she marks the grave of a couple with a Russian name
And since there are no dates carved in the base for the woman
They say
The angel was white

He was rich, he bought it for their grave, and dying, told his wife
She should not marry, or have a lover
But as she did not obey
The angel turned black

The black angel is massive, and calm, and says not a word
But in the distance, among the houses
Something flaps above the pines
Like hollow bones clacking
Tiny pennants flap moodily
Three on either side of the telephone pole

Isn't it like the river
At low water
To expose the mud flats
With such little drama

Bridge there
Built some time past
Bears
A bronze plaque that is never read
By the few who pass by
In the bright sun and that radiating heat

Eternal witness
Speaks of an early ferry
Pulled across the stream
By human arms
At this spot

Toyota monsters buzz along
In an endless stream
Over the concrete

A clear blue morning
Over the tract of weeds
By the edge of the development
I seem to sing the body geographic

I'll take you down a path
Through rain and saplings

There is a huge stone there
Standing alone
Almost hidden
Covered with moss

Unmoved in years

If a stone
Can be gentle
She is so

The stone stays as she is
Another body, in the country

O strange! Waywardness of the heart
For love knows where to draw the line
Attaching the heart to the rest
And will be there, soon enough
In body, as always, in heart

That cord and that line
Within a frame that supports the body
Heated from within
Cooled by breezes

One backbone
One of many parts
Padded by discs
Guarding a most central nerve
And feet upon the ground
A most eternal connection

A single backbone country
A land most central
Centralized in the unity of a river

The sky gathers in
                      its skirts
Cumulus cluster at the zenith
The wind enlarges as the trees explode in sound
The cottonwood speaks to us
                            in big voice
The cottonwood, in the wind, by the stream

Peace to you, O strange land
Peace to the land changed
And stripped of what pays
Peace to the people
Who respond to its weather, its texts
Its visage
This world has no corners
The horizon a perfect circle

Nameless shallow pond
On a green lawn
Behind a fence in spring
Peacefully reflecting
All that is blue

I stand in the country

Near heartbone and breastpond
Hog's back rising with its thick woods

Slight calls of birds
And the smell of fresh air

This pond a wide drop
Wider than the eye

To vanish under summer sun
Like all history, lost

When I am so overcome
With sleep as to fall
Hopefully I have stopped and taken notice of
The auspiciousness of the place

Hopefully I have cooked and eaten
Some things from the earth
When I am so overcome
With sleep as to fall

ANOTHER RIVER

The jagged outline of the world
Bluffs covered with forest
A dead tree by the shore
Branches occupied by blackbirds,
Red-winged, vigilantes of dawn
Rise and string out across the surface

Dragonflies pose over the water
Motionless in flight
As first light scatters
Then becomes present

Canoe splits the water
Shaping a course
Past the red sand gullies
Fallen logs in the water

The wind over the river will steal the leaves
And drop them here to float
Then fall to the deeps

No arguing with fall when it comes
The growing white, the silence
No stopping the transformation

THE WIRE

he strung a wire between the trees
in lieu of a fence
& wound it around each
to secure it

the trees added rings
year by year
while the wire rusted

finally it was deep within
& the fence was no more

years later another cut down a tree
to discover the core had been
blackened by the iron

the twisted wire rang
when touched by the saw

"AWAKE TO GREEN"

awake to green
and gentle cicada
voices in wave
vanish into calm

across the gully
a fresh haze
blends dark green
shadows, fair
lighter green
in the open beyond

bluejays dart
through the
overhanging foliage
the deer live
secret lives
deep in the woods

birds and crickets
awake to green
a soft breeze moves
against leaf surfaces

woodpeckers hop up
a dying tree
in search of lunch,
single leaves quiver
in a mild, continual
rain

an orchard
overgrown with ivy
awakes to green,

brightens into a greener,
paler prospect

trunks stand against
faraway light
oaks and sassafras
are revealed

the buzz of wings
overhead
brings the mind
to a greener place
the trees sway
to daybreak

THE CONCERN

Able to move through the world
from one end to another, calmly
buying milk at a bodega
or standing beneath red cliffs
watching a waterfall
amid droplets of spray

Hearing that voice
which fills my eyes, etc.
and viewing the celestial
pedestrians:
cirrus: ice crystals
nimbus: something to do with rain
cumulus: specimens of the real

Gray clouds depend
as if anchored to the earth
light spaces itself
across subjects of inherent
instability, like blossoms,
snow, sailboats, crowds

Where is
a harmony parallel to nature's?
wherein an instant is mirror smooth,
presents itself honestly,
green, then greener

In the mind there is no conclusion
positive constellations are hidden
no way to go that shouts it is the way
and effort seems to result in nothing
a sure sign that light
dispels no evil, no confusion

Around the corner some sort of future
clearly waits for those who approach
it is a canvas upon which
all men have painted
with varying results

The concern guides us
not to be false
not to catch a drift
that doesn't ring true

Nothing certain but
the pink rose mallow
extravagantly blooming
beside the stream

It is nothing but
the pleasure of color,
a trust placed
in the continuance
of a landscape

POETRY & SPEECH
for Steve Levine and Gary Lenhart

Heroic speaking without thinking
        on the streetcorner
becomes the model for poems

The beauty of cadenced speech
        in flow
proves the spur to write

Years of wondering at the complexities
        of talk falling on the ear
leads to your writing:

At the root of utterance
        a common perception
unexpressed but no less true

Unnoticed like light play
        on solar cloud arrangement
over the roofs

You know you can
        you will
glance to the heart
        & not look away

then speak
        a graph of energy
                usage shaped by intent

CORAGES

why do the willow leaves
stay greener longer
than those of any other
tree?

the constancy of the tree's
core, the heart wanting
to grow

why do its yellow leafless
branches bend so far
with the icy winds?

its longing to continue
through the cold, its firm
attachment to its place

UNTITLED

a crow, shadowbreaker
crosses sharp snow
echoes raw clouds

past wires, like birches
wind happens
shares a voice with branches

leaves wander across crust
weed clusters stiffen
tree aura marks surface

grateful for daylight
essential as breath
we share what changes
what stays

day after another
permanent as clouds
in stately motion

CLEAR THE PATH

clear the path
here comes the truth

from the community mountain
across rolling plains
the medicine grows
enough to go around

slopes from valleys run through it all
other shrubs, a tide of them, lapping
are by no means sheltered
by rocky pinnacles
but flow out, excluded, over trees
exhibiting dots and ridges
in a simple arrangement
of zones and sections

lodgepole, silver, and Jeffrey pines
the different species are found
in the deep canyons that extend from the axis
or on the upper pine belt, which sweeps up
green plants imitating
the strands of the food web

your taste
sweet medicine
it is very
beautiful

rabbitbrush, sagebrush, buckwheat,
serviceberry, granite and other gilias,
desert sweet, desert peach, wild current,
and bitterbrush
the scree jumbles are

barren of such growth
not one-twentieth of the surface
is in shade at clear noonday
you enter the lower fringe
of the forest
command superb views
of the park-like surface, strewn
with the variations in color

edge of the timber line
faceted by the numerous canyons
eroded into its face
a charm of moss attached in blue cloth
brings the forest, as a whole,
within the comprehension
above the waning sea of evergreens
the rocks of the summit peak
in a dwarfed, wavering fringe

now you cross a wild garden
next you come to the silver fir belt
a broken line of contact wavers
across the sierra
all the way
up to the storm-beaten edges
and ever and anon you emerge
through brown needles and burrs

sweet medicine
grant me two wishes

I wish there might come to me
an otter-skin quiver
I wish that I
were tall

WING

a widening ripple
of geese wing it
back north

there is a power
that draws them there

a linkage that guides them
along the flyway
in V formation

blown off course
they find their way back

as for us, there are times
we fail to see
the goals we work toward

are not simply chosen
deep within ourselves

but are resolved in dialogue
between the people we are
and the winds of consequence

plans which falter
do not fail, but change

the wise-hearted
adapt and go forth
fact to face

like these wild geese
unjarred from their aim
they could hearten the world

EXPLODED VIEW

heart's claim not shared
what to do
the manage of dark forces
becomes mine alone
the wills above (birds)
but passing premises,
like as not an owl solos:
"yeah, yeah, all right"

the last of the sky collects,
the air near our bodies
turns closer. Clouds
interblur the sun's
transit to the dark.
Crickets even the night,
an evening splintered by
a thousand lightning bugs
who listen to the owl's advice:
"yeah, yeah, all right"

MORNING SNOW

before motion disturbs
all flurries cease
pine fronds gather
aloft, powder adheres

to worn edges of trees
disguised as forms
lightly weighted
visions startling as the mind

that finds joins in the world.
Seamless, icy,
lighted, weighty,
the white crust is untracked

by wind. Particles are
now breath in clouds,
crescent windforms,
expanses, atmosphere scraps.

between patterns we see
a place coheres
real as branches
among hundreds of stars

A LETTER

I dreamt you sent me a postcard saying
"I've chosen a compulsively married person & am happy"
which seemed rather lame.
On the back was a poem
& a note announcing 38 new poems
titled "A Quart Brown Water"

I woke to the interior light of the city at dawn to write this
Blue grid combinations kept dark in the distance

Years ago, I told you about Philip Whalen's reflection on a friend
who never responded to his letters,
didn't acknowledge the books he sent him,
made Whalen feel like a planet spun into space

I never dreamt then that this would be about us,
that even the need to write could die,
that the cut would seem so final between us
as the result of no final break
but only of distance, time, & things lost

LIKE GRACIE ALLEN

I really can't pretend to attain to such genius
but the desire to build Giverny on gumbo clay,
caliche, a thin layer of soil with beaucoup rocks
approaches foolish grandeur. There exists now
a detached palazzo of pink brick and moss trim,
once an open framework you could see through,
now solid against sky & clouds, horizontalities
of bricks and shingles laid one on another.
Cascading blossoms against lush dark green leaves
enclosing a greensward dotted with trees
is a dream that has yet to displace
the disorderly biomass arrayed, tufted,
across a polygon whose corners are theoretical
and marked with small orange flags. The
purple flower clusters are weeds, *verbena
bipinnatifida*, bigger and bluer than the
seedlings carefully set out among the bark chunks.
Texas light rewards all the blooms with a
brighter interior glow.

POEM ("RURAL LIGHT...")

rural light, the lark ascending
no word as to yes or no from anyone
light catcher fastens onto the morning
transfigures a patch of ground
makes what is seen move from eye to brain to surface
& stay
a shelf of light, a tool of what is to come
some high cloudiness at nine a.m., music for strings,
percussion and celesta, clouds as software
better or not to be impalpable?
a different issue to be recallable
also a different issue to represent
art as perception recorded tells us we have not been alone
in seeing or feeling, birds intone their liquid nonsense
capacity of the single voice to entrance, to capture
forests of crickets, hidden strengths & messages
Tell me why the alignment of clouds means nothing

POEM ("A PRECURSOR TO DUSK...")

A precursor to dusk settles here. The rays lower their angle of approach.

Darkness is not yet an actor, though full sunlight no longer plays a continuing role.

Forgotten dozing businesses line the streets. Cloudware dots the skies. Suave and cerebral aristos and scoundrels walk the streets, but mostly ranchers and kickers amble beside the seared grass.

Even when indirect, the light is stark, yellow, overwhelming, not the luminist atmosphere of a Midwestern town, or the cool blue brightness in a Manhattan canyon.

A summer downpour breaks the stillness, scores it, until the form of silence changes, shifts to become something else. Traffic emits only white noise, that quickly fades into the background.

Then the rain relents, the light returns to outline the surfaces and spaces. The eyes glance up, and like a painted backdrop behind mirrored towers, a rainbow stretches over Maple Street's Mexican bars.

NATURE SYMBOLIZED

With what joy, or delight, can space be imagined and structured in the mind? There is probably some pleasure in imagining the distances between stars and trying to grasp their endlessness. Like staring into one of two mirrors that face each other, or idly looking at the bottle which bears a label depicting a man holding a bottle, on which there is a label depicting a man, the continual regression of limits in the imagining of cosmic space makes the pleasure of glimpsing this space in the mind more theoretical than real. Space has limits. The definition of spaces gives pleasure. The outline of a space's dimension defines that space. The definition of spaces distinguishes them one from another. Their physical characteristics define the pleasure we feel being inside them, perceiving their alignment and variation in surface.

In dreams we find streets become corridors, rooms become houses, cities become worlds. The fact of enclosure thus becomes more real than the size of the enclosures, or their supposed function. Nor do what we call rooms differ profoundly in their achievement, both being artifacts of culture, from what we call streets. Neither are natural. All people live near to the boundary between nature, the world not defined and ordered by people, and culture, the world that people have formed and structured. We live within reach of nature but we clearly live within culture. Even if we travel to part of the world where the hand of man has had relatively little impact we carry an envelope of culture around with us. The way we eat, the way we dress, the way we behave to one another, the way we perceive our surroundings are all artifacts of culture. Though a park or a street might enjoy natural light and the open air, as spaces they bear no less of the imprint of culture than does a room. A high mountain meadow in the Rockies, defined by sheltering peaks, untracked by roads, might have claim to being within nature, but even there we find abandoned farm machinery and tenantless cabins. The cabins rouse themselves back to being rooms when hikers spend nights there. Even a solitary traveler making his way through such a meadow cannot escape being within culture, nor would he want to do so. For culture is itself the definition of humanness.

It is the exuberance with which we perceive the limits to the spaces we encounter which gives pleasure. They frame our activities and, in a manner of speaking regulate our feelings and responses. The quiet of a museum, with ambient light flooding the space from barrel vaults above, provokes the feeling of calm and joyous perception with which we view its contents. The traditional church structure, high-ceilinged space within which light and darkness are strongly contrasted, provides a setting within which contemplation on the relation between heaven and earth or between God and man can more easily spring forth. We enclose our bedrooms, provide chambers for privacy and sleep. Each space is defined, and its limits are set forth, with the view of bringing forth a certain response from its human inhabitants. This is no less true of gardens or squares than it is of rooms, nor is it untrue for those spaces that, we may feel, dysfunctionally provoke feelings of unease or even terror rather than of calm. The response of a pedestrian along a high speed expressway is as valid, and as determined by the nature of the space within which he is enclosed, as that of the picture viewer in a gallery. It is not a place where he belongs. The noise and wind of the passing traffic, and the hard and unyielding surfaces, let him know that.

At the moment a man sits writing in an armchair in a living room.

FLOW AND ASSEMBLAGE

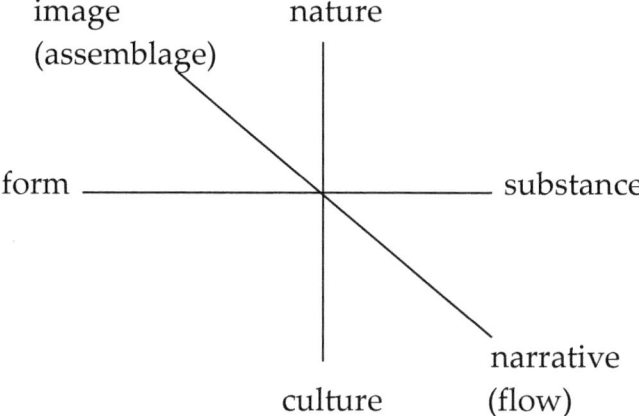

CARS

Counselled by sleep, we cross the day's transom
Trade its lighted hours for ones we ransom
Chambers dark when we leave, dark at return
The skyline orange fimbriated, handsome
For a world that doesn't care what we earn.
Down these roads speed a thousand brushing cars
Each one heedless of the fading of the stars.

Sable night enfolds us, then unravels
The sun and the drivers begin their travels
The world has planted a seed, the dawn.
Unnoticed, not the least of its marvels
Is light shining through droplets on the lawn.
Morning rays flood the fields suddenly
Outlining the day that will be.

We drive on, follow familiar ways
Minds caught by radios, thoughts of the day's
Occupations, what we do pushes aside
The sun fully borne over the blue haze.
Then this absorption yields to the light outside
As the city emerges, more real,
We become aligned with what we see and feel

TRIP HAIKU

Zen of long long drives
Monkey mind wants to make calls
Don't see half the signs

FLATTOP JOURNAL

"Chair turns and in the double mirror waver
The old man cranks me down and cracks a chuckle"
-- Gary Snyder, "Bubbs Creek Haircut"

4/12/05 First flattop haircut, yet another time

>The zen of flattops: what is
>The sound of your hair hitting the floor

4/26/05 A conversation with the barber

>Jim the customer: A high and tight flattop at my last barber's meant the hair was clipped as short as possible on the sides and back up to the point where the top begins. I'd like to look like that.

>Jim the barber: I used to do seven or eight flattops a day. And they are hard! It seemed that everyone in town had a flattop. I never thought they'd come back in style. Don't go tell all your buddies where you got it.

>Jim the customer: I don't have any buddies.

5/10/05 Staring

>Staring intently at just one thing
>Across the room at eye level
>A shelf bracket or a pattern in the wallpaper
>Sitting up straight, very still
>Both soles flat against the chair's footrest
>Both palms flat on the arms of the chair
>Head held high and level
>So the haircut might be perfectly flat

CLARK AND LOIS

Clark and Lois had breakfast, eggs
She said, "It's so hard to define
What I mean by truth."
Clark dreamt of his cape, not his rod
Rushing into a phone booth, car horns
Echoing in that little chamber

Lois looked out of the chamber
Felt deep within her the eggs
Could imagine on his forehead the horns
That she thought so divine
Clark rushed out to his hot rod
He needed to get to work, in truth

Jimmy Olson said, "Ain't it the truth
I hardly get to use my camera
Before some galoot shoves a rod
Into my chest. You can't break eggs
Without making an omelet."
Clark tried to define
Where what he heard was. Was it horns?

Far below the Daily Planet, in a bar, listening to horns
Lois thought about fishing rods
And the spark she called divine
Listening to a combo in the chamber
"What did they call those fish eggs?"
Clark stumbled in, seeking the truth

As always, it was hard to determine the truth
Caught, as it was, on dilemma's horns
Nothing as everyday as eggs.
Clark, changing in a closet, knocked down a rod,
Before flying, out the door, out of the chamber

In a way mild-mannered did not define

Lois didn't feel superman in him, couldn't define
Him as the man who leaped buildings, didn't know his
truth
Like a kangaroo court meeting in camera
Couldn't hear the whoosh of his speed over the horns
Or his electricity, like negative and positive rods
Clark sighed and went back to his eggs

No spark, nothing divine, could she see, just her eggs
She sat in the chamber, listening to the jazz horns
Which to her were the only truth. She put back the closet
rod

DREAM

In a house we were moving into
Mom was with me in a bedroom
I had to get stuff from other rooms, I didn't have the right things
She was getting up, I was afraid she'd fall
Rehab people came to do exercises with her
One lady said she was from Duwamish, Washington
In the building was a big bar. We are in Houston
A waitress said that hers and my poetry books were finalists for a prize
I sit down at a table with a drink and several people
I look at the book – it has photos from the family tree, sometimes funny juxtapositions with the poems
Looking out of the window of the house we were living in
Dee Dee shows up with two cops in cruisers
The perpetrators have neatly covered the house and yard and all the items around it
And the house of the neighbors as well, all over, with small logs, carefully stacked
A mob of people are watching and talking about this from the street
In a store, buying shoes for mom, with her there with me
I tell the clerk she is dead. He looks doubtful, and confused
The family tree has become a book of poems – a poem for each person
Sometimes the people have written them, sometimes I have written them
I meet with some of the relatives, I don't know them, and they are nonchalant
About the poems they have written and about sharing them with me

CHANT DE BÉNONI AUDET

Je travaille avec mon père et mes frères à la ferme et à la pêche
Je prends le train et je voyage loin. J'abats les vieux arbres
J'aime ma petite Irlandaise
And I love my children, girls and boys, growing up around me
I work, I live, I love life, I love my family
I will always be the man I always was
Je serai toujours l'homme que j'ai toujours été

translation:
I work with my father and brothers on the farm and fishing
I take the train and travel far away. I cut down the old trees
I love my little Irish girl

and the last line repeats the previous English line

I will always be the man I always was

THE POEM ABOUT CLOUDS IS FINISHED, I THINK

Clouds rampant on a field azure, clouds argent,
Shadows under them – whatever grey is in heraldic language – cendrée
They rise up into the sky from left to right over the freeway as I drive
It's spring – earliest spring – the spring of light before the fresh green of spring appears
Today is my mother's birthday, the first one since she died.
Why is it that while I drive I feel bereft? I feel her loss more strongly than at any other time.
More often than not I get in the car, single-minded, to drive somewhere to accomplish some errand
And suddenly my eyes fill with tears and my mind fills with sadness because she isn't there
What is it about being alone behind the wheel that differs from being alone anywhere else?
Blinking tears away to see the road, waiting for the moment of bereavement to recede
Why do I feel like this and when will it get better?
And wouldn't she say if she were here, "Robin, don't be sad. It'll be all right,"
Just like she spent my whole life saying whenever something went wrong and I came to her with it.

MYSTERIOUS BARRICADES

My dreams are full of physical complexity
Museums with apartments inside them
Office complexes with hardware stores
Parking in front and in back
Vendors who couldn't provide packaging
But who can now, at a reasonable price

Then I wake up, and consciousness of
A different sort intrudes
The first thing I notice is the high ringing sound
In my ear, it's always a surprise
To find it there again, hello old friend
I acknowledge its presence, then I get up
And I continue